Safari Animals™
Animales de safari™

ELEPHANTS
ELEFANTES

Amelie von Zumbusch

Traducción al español: Ma. Pilar Sanz

PowerKiDS press & **Editorial Buenas Letras**™

New York

Published in 2007 by The Rosen Publishing Group, Inc.
29 East 21st Street, New York, NY 10010

First Edition

Book Design: Erica Clendening
Layout Design: Julio Gil and Lissette González

Photo Credits: Cover, pp. 1, 5, 7, 9, 11, 15, 19, 24 (bottom left, bottom right) © Digital Vision; p. 13, 17, 23, 24 (top right) © Artville; pp. 21, 24 (top left) © Digital Stock.

Cataloging Data

Zumbusch, Amelie von.
  Elephants-Elefantes / Amelie von Zumbusch: traducción al español Ma. Pilar Sanz — 1st ed.
      p. cm. — (Safari animals-Animales de safari)
  Includes index.
  ISBN-13: 978-1-4042-7605-5 (library binding)
  ISBN-10: 1-4042-7605-X (library binding)
  1. Elephants—Juvenile literature. 2. Spanish language materials. I. Title.

Manufactured in the United States of America

CONTENTS

CONTENIDO

The African elephant is
a large animal. It has
gray skin.

El elefante africano es un
animal muy grande. El
elefante africano tiene la
piel gris.

African elephants live
in the forests and open
lands of Africa.

Los elefantes africanos
viven en las selvas y las
sabanas de África.

7

The African elephant is the largest land animal that lives on Earth. It can weigh as much as 14,000 pounds (6,350 kg).

El elefante africano es el animal terrestre más grande del planeta. Estos elefantes pueden pesar hasta 14,000 libras (6,350 kg.).

Elephants have long teeth called tusks. An elephant's tusks keep growing during its whole life.

Los elefantes tienen grandes dientes llamados colmillos. Los colmillos siguen creciendo durante toda la vida del elefante.

An elephant's long nose is called a trunk.

A la enorme nariz de los elefantes se le llama trompa.

These elephants are
drinking from a water hole.
Elephants use their trunks
to drink.

Estos elefantes toman
agua de una charca. Los
elefantes usan sus trompas
para tomar agua.

15

Elephants eat plants. One elephant eats more than 100 pounds (45 kg) of plants in one day.

Los elefantes comen plantas. Un solo elefante puede comer más de 100 libras (45 kg) de plantas en un día.

Elephants live in family groups. These groups are made up of children, mothers, and grandmothers.

Los elefantes viven en grupos de familias. En estas familias hay mamás, abuelitas y elefantitos.

A baby elephant is called a calf.

Al elefante bebé se le llama cría de elefante.

Adult elephants teach an elephant calf many things. Elephants learn easily. They are smart animals.

Los elefantes les enseñan muchas cosas a sus crías. Los bebés aprenden rápido. Son animales muy listos.

Words to Know / Palabras que debes saber

calf / (la) cría

trunk / (la) trompa

tusk / (el) colmillo

water hole / (la) charca

Index

Índice